C334127008

An Introduction to Coping with

Eating Problems

2nd Edition

Gillian Todd

ROBINSON

First published in Great Britain in 2017 by Robinson

1 3 5 7 9 10 8 6 4 2

A CIP catalogue record for this book is available from the British Library.

Important note

This book is not intended as a substitute for medical advice or treatment. Any person with a condition requiring medical attention should consult a qualified medical practitioner or suitable therapist.

ISBN: 978-1-47213-850-7

Typeset in Bembo by Initial Typesetting Services, Edinburgh
Printed and bound in Great Britain by Clays Ltd, St Ives plc.

Papers used by Robinson are from well-managed forests and other responsible sources.

Robinson
An imprint of
Little, Brown Book Group
Carmelite House
50 Victoria Embankment
London EC4Y 0DZ

An Hachette UK Company
www.hachette.co.uk

www.littlebrown.co.uk

www.overcoming.co.uk

Contents

About This Book

Most of us feel unhappy with our appearance at some time or another, especially during our teenage years when our bodies begin to change. Some of us become happier as we get older and become more accepting of ourselves as we develop a wider sense of perspective. Unfortunately, though, this is not the case for all of us, and sometimes those very normal concerns about our weight and body shape don't improve and become the sole focus of attention. Many of us choose to diet, of course, but sometimes this may spill over and become prolonged and extreme. Instead of us controlling what we eat, the diet (or other things we do to control our weight) begins to control us, and then becomes very important to us. This may happen when a person believes their entire self-worth is based on their ability to control food and eating or their weight and body shape. And when restricting food becomes so ultra-important, along with concerns over weight and body shape, this can become an 'eating disorder'.

This book aims to help those of us who have these kinds of problems with eating – and it also aims to help our families and friends understand a bit about what's going on. It's an introduction to overcoming issues – with food, eating and body image – and will help you make a start on your journey to recovery.

Part 1 describes the symptoms of eating disorders; Part 2 looks at practical steps you can take and skills you can use to deal with the issues, including a few written exercises you can complete, with examples to guide you. You'll also find a chapter for family and friends that addresses some of the common concerns they might have. Many people find it helpful to read and work through the book from start to finish and, at first, you may also find it useful to make notes as you go along.

When you have problems with eating and dieting you can feel so trapped in patterns of thinking and behaving that it might be difficult to believe you'll ever get better. But a majority of people with eating disorders do get better, or at least make great improvements. You can improve, too, by learning how to do something about it. Recovery can be very difficult and take a long time but, if you continue to work on it, this book will help you address these concerns. Keep at it! Every step you take – no matter how small – is a positive step in the right direction. Setbacks are common and expected but they are something we learn from and that make us stronger.

During this recovery process, many of us will need the support of our family and friends. This is a good thing. The right kind of support is a vital part of recovery, and it's important for everyone who's involved. No one's expecting immediate changes or an instant turnaround. But, if you've given it a try and make less progress than you'd hoped to, or if making changes feels too overwhelming, it may be best to go your family doctor and discuss what alternatives are available. That is also a step on the road to recovery. Your doctor may recommend a qualified therapist or specialist and this may be more helpful for you. Every situation is unique, and it is important that you find the solution that is best for you.

Gillian Todd

Part 1: UNDERSTANDING EATING DISORDERS

1

What are Eating Disorders?

Eating disorders are complex and distressing psychological conditions that are common in young women aged between fifteen and twenty-four. Although the majority of sufferers are female, one in ten people with an eating disorder is male. Eating disorders can affect men and women of all ages, from all races and socio-economic backgrounds, sexual orientation, body shapes and weights.

People may not recognise they have an eating disorder or often try to hide their eating disorder because they feel ashamed and guilty about their behaviour. They fear being misunderstood and worry that their friends and family will be dismissive, critical or reject them if they are found out. Often by the time someone seeks help for an eating disorder they will have lived with their problem for many years.

Eating disorders generally fall into four broad categories: anorexia nervosa; bulimia nervosa; binge eating disorder; and something known as 'Other

Specified Feeding and Eating Disorder' (OSFED) which covers a whole host of different presentations of eating problems. People with anorexia nervosa try to restrict or avoid food whenever possible but, as a result, they become so engrossed with thoughts about food and eating that they find it difficult to think about anything else. And whereas most of us tend to think of fruit and vegetables as 'good' and healthy – part of our 'Five a Day' – and so-called 'junk' food such as crisps or sweets as 'bad' and unhealthy, many people with anorexia have increasingly strict rules about what they will allow themselves to eat. As they limit their food choices, and how many calories they will allow themselves to eat, their list of what they consider to be 'bad' food becomes longer, even if it includes fruit and vegetables.

People with anorexia feel extremely anxious about their weight, and are overly concerned and fearful of becoming fat even when underweight, and this is why they control and limit food and eating to this extreme. They lose perspective, and feel and sense they or specific body parts are fat no matter how low their weight is or what they see in the mirror. Once anorexia takes hold, the drive to be thin takes over any other thought. Unfortunately, even when the person with anorexia becomes extremely underweight, they still feel it is necessary to lose even more weight and this can become dangerous very quickly. It is also very upsetting for family and friends of the person suffering from anorexia, who may often brush aside and dismiss any concerns others may have about their behaviour, even when they begin to feel physically unwell. The desire to lose weight takes precedence over anything else.

People with bulimia nervosa also have an overwhelming fear of becoming fat, even though most people with bulimia are a healthy weight. Like those people suffering from anorexia, those with bulimia spend a lot of time thinking about their body weight and their body shape, and this then affects their ability to eat normally. People with bulimia tend to alternate between periods of extreme dieting and periods of binge eating, which usually involves eating a very large amount of food quickly and in secret. Crucially, when people with bulimia begin to eat they don't feel they have the ability to stop themselves. Once the binge is over, they tend to feel overfull and even more anxious than before and then feel absolutely petrified they will gain weight. They try to undo this feeling by getting rid of (or 'purging') food from their body by making themselves sick or by using laxatives.

People with Binge Eating Disorder (BED) – which shouldn't be confused with bulimia nervosa – binge eat regularly over a long period, for at least six months and at least twice a week, but do not purge themselves. Because they don't make themselves sick, they regularly take in more calories than their body actually needs and tend to become overweight. This, in turn, leads many people with BED to feel bad about themselves and often misunderstood. As with bulimia, a person with binge-eating disorder feels out of control and powerless to stop eating – it isn't just a case of having more willpower. And we've all got to remember that our emotions often affect how we eat. For example, when we're stressed or upset, some of us will eat more and some of us will eat less. People with binge-eating disorder eat more, and find that this becomes a form of comfort or relief from a problematic situation. It is often a way of avoiding difficult feelings or the circumstances that surround them or cause them in the first place.

The majority of people with eating disorders fall into the category known as OSFED. What this means is that they aren't strictly anorexic, bulimic or BED; but those who suffer from eating disorders in this wider category still require as much care and attention as those who suffer specifically from anorexia nervosa or bulimia nervosa. There is no sharp boundary between the different types of eating disorders because they tend to share some of the same symptoms and features. It's also common for the nature of an eating disorder to change over time.

Let's take a look now at some examples of people with different kinds of eating disorders:

Rachel's Story

Rachel is a 22-year-old journalist who was 14 years old when she was diagnosed with an eating disorder. When her family had moved to London, she found it difficult to settle into her new school and was bullied by a group of older girls who teased her about her weight, even though it was completely normal for her age. One girl posted rude comments about her on Facebook and Twitter. As a result of the bullying, she felt self-conscious of her figure and believed that if she lost a bit of weight the others would like her and she'd feel better about herself. She believed that if she lost weight and felt in control that the bullying wouldn't hurt her.

Rachel first began skipping breakfast and cutting out fatty and sugary food. After a while, she began to receive compliments about her appearance and this gave her a sense of achievement. She also found that controlling what she ate helped distract her from feeling lonely and upset at school. But then she started to become obsessed with food and eating and couldn't think about or concentrate on anything else. This also upset her; however, she was unable to stop herself or her behaviour and so continued to limit what she ate and then lost even more weight, to the point where she could see the outline of her ribs and shoulder bones. Although it upset her on the one hand, being able to deny herself food also made her feel strong, in control and protected, even though she was continually hungry. She later referred to these feelings as her 'anorexia bubble', which she described as an invisible shield – no matter how mean anyone was towards her, she could not feel hurt.

Although one side of her recognised that she was thin, there was another side that still made her feel overweight and made her believe that her stomach was 'huge' or fat. She noticed that her attitude to food had become pretty much inflexible because she was only able to stick to a certain and strict routine of eating and would check her weight several times a day. She stopped seeing friends outside of school and shut herself away in her bedroom.

As her diet continued and she became extremely thin, she began constantly to feel cold, her hair started to fall out and her periods stopped. Her mood was usually low and she felt depressed much of the time. Rachel's family were so worried that her mum made an appointment for them both to see the family doctor, who referred Rachel to a specialist at an eating-disorder unit where they helped her gain weight and deal with the reasons why she'd developed the eating disorder in the first place.

But getting better was a challenge and very difficult; for example, when people told her she looked well, Rachel believed that meant she looked fat. So she would immediately start to diet again and vow only to eat foods she thought wouldn't make her put weight on. She'd skip breakfast again, throw her packed lunch away at school and eat very little during family mealtimes. She constantly felt ravenously hungry, and began to raid the fridge or eat large amounts of food quickly and in secret. She found that once she started to eat she felt unable to stop until she felt completely bloated. When it came to food and eating she felt conflicted: one side of her felt guilt when she ate and she would worry about gaining weight, the other side of her enjoyed eating, which she found comforting and made her feel better. Her binges were triggered by a variety of things: boredom; difficult situations; even feeling fat. After bingeing, she'd picture the food she'd just eaten sitting in her stomach and would feel the urge to get rid of it in order to wipe the slate clean. As a result, she began to make herself sick to feel less guilty and worried about her weight, yet it exhausted her – both physically and mentally – and she'd beat herself up for having lost control, which made her feel even worse. Rachel would eventually reach a point of feeling so out of control with the bingeing that she'd go back to severe dieting. She's followed this pattern for the past eight years.

Megan's Story

Megan is a 19-year-old student nurse who developed an eating disorder about 2 years ago. She found she was eating a lot of 'junk' food and so decided to go on a healthy-eating diet. She restricted the type of food she ate and cut out what she considered to be 'bad' food. She gradually lost weight over a period of about nine months until she'd become so thin that her periods stopped and she felt physically unwell – her joints ached and she was constantly tired and cold.

Megan didn't recognise that she had a problem and, in fact, tried not to think about what was happening to her. She rarely checked her weight or scrutinised her body and, when the subject came up among friends or family, she denied actively trying to lose weight. And when her friends and family eventually told her they were concerned, she felt they were over-reacting; however, she often felt fat or believed that parts of her body were too big.

One day at work and completely out of the blue, a colleague told Megan that she was too skinny. This came as a huge shock to Megan, who'd convinced herself that she looked perfectly fine. It was such a shock that it made her think again about how she looked and then, after sleeping on it for a few nights, she decided to ask for help. This took a lot of courage and she almost didn't go once or twice but she psyched herself up, asked a friend to go with her and made it to the appointment on time.

Megan's doctor referred her to a cognitive behavioural therapist, who helped her to learn to eat normally again and to deal with distressing thoughts about food, eating and her weight as well as problematic behaviours. She found the treatment difficult at first and often thought about stopping but, with the support of her family and friends, she gradually made a full recovery.

Rupert's Story

Rupert is an 18-year-old university student who's had an eating disorder for the last 5 months. He was anxious about going away to university and found adjusting to living away from home harder than he thought it would be. He had difficulty finding new friends and didn't feel he fitted in to the right groups.

His day would typically start with a cooked breakfast from the canteen, then waffles, ice cream and a milk shake in the café. He would wander around town discreetly buying food to binge on to ensure that nobody noticed and he'd eat a large Cornish pasty and jacket potato with cheese and beans. He would feel a sense of euphoria in anticipation of eating and during a binge he would feel calm and relaxed. However, once he'd finished eating, feelings of panic would set in and he felt terrified of gaining weight and he'd make himself sick.

He felt lonely and began to comfort himself with sweets, guilty and worried about gaining weight. He discovered that making himself sick after eating would make him feel better temporarily and so he got into the habit of binge eating whenever he felt bored or lonely. He would often binge and then vomit instead of studying or going to classes. Very quickly after vomiting he'd feel hungry again and on his way back home he'd buy chocolate, cakes and biscuits from the supermarket so that he could continue to binge in the privacy of his room. Once he'd finished all the food he'd bought he'd make himself sick again, and only at that point would he start studying, which was usually late in the evening. He'd convince himself he would stop bingeing and would sometimes manage to go without doing so for two days before starting all over again.

Jaya's Story

Jaya is a 38-year-old, second-generation Indian British woman. She is married with two children and works part-time as an administrator in a bank. Her problems with binge eating started during childhood and she recalls raiding the cupboards and hoarding food in her room, which she would binge on. After gaining too much weight, she was put on a diet, which made her feel controlled by others and self-conscious about eating in front of others; her bingeing then escalated.

This pattern of alternating between dieting and binge eating continued throughout her life. Jaya described herself as an 'all-or-nothing' person: she would 'detox' with vegetable juice for a week followed by binge eating several times a day on confectionery. During a binge, she would frantically stuff food into her mouth and eat rapidly as if in a trance until she could eat no more. Immediately following a binge, she would feel ashamed and remorseful and vow to stop; as the pattern continued, she became more critical of herself and her mood was low.

Weight and Body Shape, and the Key Symptoms of Eating Disorders

Most of us feel dissatisfied with our body weight and shape at some point in our lives. This is especially true for young women in the year after they've had their first period, when it's common to gain weight. Why? Well, during late childhood our hormones change, and this triggers a growth spurt. For girls, this can start as early as the age of ten and usually reaches its peak by about fifteen, but there are, of course, exceptions to the rule with early developers or late bloomers. As a girl's height increases, sex hormones are produced by the ovaries and change her appearance – she goes from having the shape of a young girl to having the body of a woman. As human bodies grow quickly at this stage they need a high amount of energy – food – much more than fully grown adults need. And after this time of rapid growth, less food is needed; however, if developing teenagers continue to eat the same amount then they run the risk of gaining too much weight. During this period and afterwards, many of us may begin to feel concerned about our appearance and develop a negative body image.

It is normal for young women to aspire to be valued; however, we live in a culture that values slimness and with a media that reinforces this with images that influence the way we think about ourselves.

For most of us there is a mismatch between how we'd like to look and how we actually are and, for many young women, putting on weight or having a negative body image is likely to affect their self-confidence and self-esteem. And while most of us experience these very normal concerns about our body image in our teenage years, these feelings often go away or become less important after we become more used to our body's new shape.

Young men are very different. During their growth spurt, they usually lose body fat and become more muscular, which many men prefer to being thin and which, in turn, boosts their self-confidence and self-esteem. However, many men are dissatisfied with their appearance and aspire to develop a lean muscular V-shaped physique, associated with masculinity and the 'ideal' male.

But regardless of whether we are male or female, these periods of change affect our feelings of our self-worth if we judge ourselves in terms of our body weight and shape and our ability to control our appetites. But they may not affect our feelings so much if we judge ourselves in terms of other things such as our performance at work, our friendships or any skills we have in a particular area. For example, Rachel believed she could only feel good about herself if she was a size 8 and weighed less than

50kg. If she weighed more than that she regarded it as a sign of weakness and a loss of self-control, and so saw herself as a failure. If we take Megan as an example, we'd find that she believed that if her thighs were fat she'd be unattractive and unlovable, even though there were so many other attractive and lovable things about her – such as her talents as a nurse and her good sense of humour. But, like other people with eating disorders, she didn't believe it when someone would praise or compliment her, and she would often refer to her body as disgusting and gross – sometimes in a jokey manner – because she was self-conscious about her weight.

What Is the Impact of Worrying about Your Weight and Shape?

People with eating disorders tend to have exaggerated concerns about their appearance and can spend hours agonising over small changes in their weight and body shape and analysing the reasons for the change. Usually, and despite reasonable explanations such as fluid retention before a period, or bloating following eating, people with eating disorders usually come to the conclusion that they've put on weight permanently. This makes them feel panicked, out of control and even more preoccupied with eating, weight and shape, and leads them to plan how to lose the weight they think they've gained. People with eating disorders often weigh themselves several times a day, even cross-checking their weight on different scales. Others avoid weighing themselves altogether because they don't want to have their fear that they've gained weight confirmed. Either way, they spend a great deal of time focusing and worrying solely on their weight, body shape, food and eating. Most of us find that the more we worry about something, the bigger the worry becomes, and then the more worried we feel. The same is true for people with eating disorders.

People with eating disorders are often preoccupied with specific parts of their body and develop another unhelpful habit that involves checking for small changes in their weight and shape. For example, Megan liked to be able to see the outline of her ribs and hip bones and would constantly check the appearance of her stomach. She'd squeeze and pinch the skin on her stomach and would do this sitting down and standing up so she could make sure there was almost no fat when she sat down. She'd also measure her waist and check her profile in the mirror several times a day. But the more she checked her body, the worse she felt about it. Because people with eating disorders tend to focus on the parts of their body they don't like, rather than their whole body, the disliked part tends to be seen out of proportion, and any flaws are magnified in the mind's eye. In contrast to this are the people who simply assume they look fat and go out of their way to avoid seeing their bodies altogether.

Obsessively checking your body in response to feeling fat and/or avoiding looking at your body will almost always lead you to become more dissatisfied with it. You may notice what you consider to be imperfections in your weight and body shape that you were not previously aware of. We know there is a relationship between body checking and reducing food intake in women with anorexia – 'the more you check, the less you eat' principle. This is even more likely to be the case if you make negative comparisons between your body shape and the body shape of people whom you consider to be thinner or more attractive than you.

Moreover, comparing how you feel you look in your mind's eye compared to how you would like to look in an ideal world is likely to make you feel more unhappy with how you look. Often driven by images in the media, and aspiring to look a particular way, this is known as our 'thin ideal', which we hold in our minds and which causes us to feel conflicted about how we feel we look and how we would like to see ourselves. Making these comparisons increases dissatisfaction with our bodies and reinforces unhealthy dieting and other eating disordered behaviours.

We also know that people who participate in 'fat talk' are more likely to become more dissatisfied with their bodies, which is more harmful than just hearing it. Fat talk – often practised by groups of women – is when they talk about their bodies in a derogatory way and make it very clear that being thin is important and something they value highly in themselves and others. For example, 'I'm so fat, my muffin top is spilling over my jeans, it's disgusting' ... 'I look like a giant sausage in this dress with all this chub' ... 'my thighs are enormous' ... and so on. Fat talk elevates the importance of the thin ideal.

Concerns about your weight and shape can have a negative impact on your relationships with other people. If you feel self-conscious about your appearance, you may find that these feelings are much worse when you're in a social situation, such as going to a party, especially where food and eating is involved. It is common to feel anxious before going to a social event but, if you have an eating disorder, you might find it even more difficult or stressful and spend a long time choosing what to wear before going out so that you can hide particular areas of your body. You may feel self-conscious and the centre of attention, as if all eyes are on you, and fear being judged negatively in terms of your weight and shape. Megan dreaded going out with her girlfriends whom she considered to be thinner and more attractive than she was. She convinced herself that if she ate any food in front of them, they'd see her as fat and greedy, or that other people would see her as fat and greedy in comparison. In the end, she found going out so upsetting and unenjoyable that she started to avoid seeing her friends, but this in turn made her feel alone and isolated.

And if you find it difficult to go out with friends, you may find it extraordinarily difficult to deal with more intimate relationships. You may find being touched by other people upsetting and start to avoid situations where this might happen. You might feel so self-conscious about your body that you avoid undressing in public places and in front of your partner. In addition, when your weight is very low, you may find that you lose your sex drive and so find yourself either avoiding intimate relationships or going along with a sexual relationship only to please your partner.

What Is a Healthy Weight?

The Body Mass Index, or BMI, is now the most accepted method for finding out if someone is a medically healthy weight or if they're overweight or underweight. It shows, in most cases, an estimate of body fat levels based on height and weight measurements. For those of you who like maths, the formula for calculating BMI is:

> Weight (kg) ÷ [height (m)]^2
>
> Your weight in kilograms is divided by your height in metres squared.
>
> For example: if your weight is 56kg, and your height is 1.65m, then the calculation is:
> 56 ÷ (1.65 x 1.65) = BMI of 20.5.

You can also use online BMI calculators such as this one: *www.cdc.gov*, and put BMI into the search engine. This site has child, teen and adult BMI calculators and it's important to use the right one for your age group. BMI is calculated in exactly the same way for teenagers and adults, but the way in which you make sense of the results takes into consideration your age and gender. The reason why we need to take age into account when interpreting the meaning of a young person's BMI is that body fat changes with age; for example, girls who have not started their periods will have a lower BMI than girls the same age who have. It also considers the variation between the body fat of boys and girls.

Bear in mind that BMI is an initial guide only, and doesn't take into account individual differences, so a super-fit athlete could fall in the overweight BMI range because muscle weighs more than fat. Here is a chart that tells you what the ranges of BMI generally mean. Remember that it is just a guide for what is considered to be a medically healthy weight:

BMI	What Does This Mean?
17.5 or below	If your weight falls within this range you are seriously underweight and need to seek medical help. You are very likely to experience some physical, psychological and social problems at this weight.
17.6–18.9	You are significantly underweight and are likely to notice the effects of being this low weight. In the Western world, very few people are able to maintain this level of BMI without seriously cutting back and restricting what they allow themselves to eat.

19–19.9	This is considered to be a low weight but healthy. It is unlikely you will experience any bad effects on your health.
20–24.9	This is considered to be a medically healthy weight.
25–29.9	This is considered to be an overweight range that is associated with an increase in physical health problems. You might consider losing a few kilos.
30 or above	This is considered to be an obese weight range that is associated with greater risk of health problems. As with those in the underweight range of 17.5 and below, you should seek medical help. For many of us the word 'obese' has a negative meaning, but it is actually a medical reference point and not intended to be a criticism.

Asian men and women – particularly from southern Asia (Indian, Pakistan, Bangladesh, Sri Lanka, Maldives and Afghanistan) – are more likely to experience health problems at a lower BMI compared to European people of the same age, sex and BMI. The reason is that Asian people tend to carry more body fat, so their normal healthy BMI range is between 18.5 and 23. According to the World Health Organisation (WHO), people from Asian cultures are medically healthier with a lower BMI than their Western counterparts. BMI guidelines for Asian people are interpreted in the following way:

less than 16 = severely underweight;
16–16.9 = moderately underweight;
16.9–18.5 = underweight;
18.5–24.9 = healthy weight;
25–29.9 = overweight;
more than 30 = obese.

How Does Worrying about My Weight Affect My Eating Habits?

Many of us try to be aware of what and when we eat as a way of making sure our weight stays fairly stable. But this becomes something different when it tips over into keeping a close eye on it all the time and controlling what and when you eat. Being able to resist eating food that most other people enjoy, or being able to eat extremely small amounts of food at a meal is something that makes people with eating disorders feel good about themselves. They see such close control of what they eat or don't eat as a sign of having strength and willpower. People with eating disorders tend to set themselves strict rules about what they can eat, when they can eat and how much they can eat. Many people choose to count calories and often subscribe to apps that calculate this for them to make sure they don't over-eat, or make sure they don't consume all their calorie allowance too early in the day in order to prevent themselves from feeling ravenously hungry later. What usually happens is that people tend to err on the side of caution and, through guessing the amount of food and calories eaten, tend to think they have eaten more than they actually have. Some people tend to take more extreme measures such as weighing and measuring the food they're going to eat. This can take up a lot of time and constantly adding up the number of calories can be frustrating and upsetting because people find they are unable to switch off this pattern of thinking. People who suffer from eating disorders often believe they need to be thinking about food and meal planning all the time to keep their eye on the ball and prevent them from gaining weight. They fear losing control and believe if they do they will keep on gaining weight.

The thought of changing these behaviours is scary, which is understandable, but it's an endless cycle – the more you feel the need to be in control, the more out of control you'll feel, which leads to doing more things that make you feel in control. And, again, the idea of being in control is very strict, so the slightest hint of feeling out of control is distressing. It was this way for Rachel who had a rule about only eating vegetables. When she managed to stick to this plan she felt in control but, if she deviated only slightly, she believed she had blown her diet and would feel out of control and upset, and would often binge eat as a way of coping with these distressing feelings, only to start the diet cycle once more.

Dieting

After puberty many of us choose to diet in order to lose weight and improve our body image. This is especially true for young women and men. Men might take up exercise such as weightlifting to increase muscle tone and bulk. This is a time when body dissatisfaction is high, especially with their thighs, bottom, hips, waist, stomach and legs. However, we know that children as young as six worry about their weight and want to be thin; by the age of ten, 80 per cent have been on at least one diet and, for many, this pattern continues throughout life. Three-quarters of women between the ages of 25 and 45 have unhealthy attitudes in relation to their bodies and food and eating, of which two-thirds are trying to lose weight.

People begin to diet for a variety of reasons; we are all exposed to the media portrayal of 'ideal' beauty and the importance of being thin. Valuing thinness is equated with beauty, and success and health is something most of us aspire to. Eating disorders are not directly caused by the cultural value of thinness in the Western world though socio-cultural pressure to be thin may play a part. Feeling dissatisfied with your body and considering yourself to be fat, or feeling fat, can lead to dieting. Other factors include observing parents dieting, or being criticised for your weight and encouraged to diet by others. Peer group endorsement of dieting, weight-related sports and being teased because of your weight may also play a part.

Dieting is different from person to person, but people with eating disorders engage in extreme attempts to limit their food intake and keep this behaviour going for some time (although binge eating disorder is the exception). They set highly specific and demanding rules for themselves that are difficult to follow all the time. Megan had two lists of food – those she considered to be good, nutritional and healthy, and those she considered to be bad. Over time, the list of 'bad' food became longer. Another of her rules involved eating exactly the same food each day at exactly the same time; for example, at breakfast she would have one sachet of porridge with a teaspoon of goji berries and 15g of blueberries with a strict measure of skimmed milk. If the berries weren't available or if there was only semi-skimmed milk in the refrigerator, she wouldn't eat at all. For lunch, she would have a shop-bought edamame bean salad and 200ml of coconut water but, if this wasn't available, she would brood over what to eat and feel too anxious to eat an alternative option despite feeling really hungry. Likewise, Rupert would set himself a maximum limit of 1,000 calories per day and used an app to plan his food for the day, which excluded carbs, fat and dairy.

Megan and Rupert and many other people with eating disorders find they adjust their life according to their diet, no matter how strict it becomes. Rachel, who needs to eat socially as part of her work, tells people she's vegan (even though she's not), so that all food options are discussed with her in advance, which makes her feel in control. Megan will only go to restaurants where she has been able to check out the menu in advance and calculate the calories.

People with eating disorders often describe thinking continually about food and eating most waking hours to the point of being distracted from other things; some prefer to eat alone, so they can either follow an eating ritual that may include cutting food into small pieces and eating very slowly or feel less self-conscious and can concentrate on what they are doing, especially when binge eating. This, in turn, increases their preoccupation with food and eating. People who are underweight find that, as they lose weight, the more they think about food and eating – to the point of obsession. Megan would spend hours in the supermarket and feel overwhelmed with the choices. She would carefully read all the food labels and struggle to make any decision about what to eat, and would often leave the shop empty-handed.

What Is Binge Eating?

Binge eating usually involves an episode of consuming a very large amount of food, usually 1,000–2,000 calories (equal to about four to eight medium-sized chocolate bars) but can range anywhere between three and thirty times the amount of food normally consumed in a day. Some people exceed more than 20,000 calories a day when they are binge eating, and those who tend to have greater binges tend to have a higher body weight. Each episode usually takes place within a time period of less than two hours. Some people will have several binges over the course of a day.

Most people binge eat in private and more often than not there is an element of planning that goes into preparing for a binge. Jaya would go to the corner shop and buy large quantities of confectionery to binge on, usually in the evening after work; she didn't trust herself to have much food in her cupboards and would go out to buy things for dinner but, once in the shop, she couldn't resist the temptation to buy packets of sweets and biscuits. Sometimes, Jaya would order two or three large takeaways from different food outlets and eat the lot. Jaya would drive to several different shops to buy food to binge on because she felt self-conscious and was worried that the shopkeeper would know she was going to binge. And occasionally, binge eaters will cook food to feed a crowd then end up eating the whole lot in one go. Rupert would buy sweets from a vending machine and eat them in his room very quickly.

People who binge tend to think they eat things high in fat and sugar – the type of food they wouldn't normally include in their diet. However, scientists who have studied what people eat during a binge have found that the foods actually consumed are for the most part high in carbohydrates such as bread, pasta and rice, and high in protein such as meat, fish, poultry and dairy products. Some people will eat almost anything, including frozen food and baby food and will, in extreme circumstances, retrieve food from the bin. Most people who are bulimic will select food on the basis of how easy it is to swallow and how easy it is to vomit up. Usually, eating takes place in secret or discreetly in public, as with Rupert.

The start of a binge is often frantic and food is consumed quickly but, as the binge progresses, the pace of eating slows down, especially if people feel confident they will not be disturbed. A sense of loss of control over eating is experienced during these episodes, and people feel unable to stop once they have started but, when they do eventually, it is for a variety of reasons, including intense physical discomfort, feelings of nausea or the fact that the food simply runs out. Jaya would stop when she ran out of money to buy more food or when the food she had been eating began to travel up her oesophagus to her throat, preventing her from eating anything else. Some people try to control the binge by setting a time limit, or will stop if they are interrupted.

People usually feel regretful and often feel distressed about having binged and will promise themselves they won't do it again and will go on a strict diet. But they rarely keep their promise. Bingeing can occur once or twice a week or several times a day. Some people report continuous binge eating for days and weeks.

Why Do People Binge Eat?

Bingeing tends to take place for a variety of reasons, such as extreme dieting, feeling stressed about a situation, or feeling uncomfortable with your body. Extreme dieting can lead people to become ravenously hungry, and the urge to satisfy the hunger overwhelms the need to have control over eating. Many people who binge say they feel upset, tense and anxious before an episode, which they believe brings a kind of momentary relief to these feelings and helps them cope with negative emotions. It's common to hear: 'Eating will comfort me' ... 'Eating is my way of zoning out – when I eat I don't have to think of anything' ... 'Eating helps me escape from my problems'.

However, some people binge when they feel bored or through craving a particular food. When Rachel felt fat, even though her weight hadn't actually changed, it would trigger a binge; Rupert would binge when he was feeling anxious and worried about his course work, but he would also binge if he felt bored. Jaya was under a lot of pressure at work and binged most evenings after her evening meals. These feelings are what we'd call trigger signals, because they set off an episode of bingeing. People often say that when they binge they notice a feeling of emotional numbness and feel detached to the point of being no longer aware of their thoughts and emotions; this can be a great relief, but only in the short term.

During these episodes, there is an internal conflict going on in people's minds – two streams of thought coexist at the same time: sufferers feel convinced that eating is a good idea; but they also think that bingeing is a bad idea and will make them feel worse. 'Should I? Shouldn't I?' And in order to deal with this, people who binge begin to give themselves pep talks, giving themselves permission to binge and justifying to themselves that this is a good idea. Rupert would say to himself, 'This is the last time I will binge ... I'll get back on track tomorrow'; Jaya would think to herself, 'I've got no willpower anyway, so go for it, you can't help it,' ... 'Eating will help me cope.' Other types of permissive thoughts might include, 'I've had a bad day and deserve something nice.' Thoughts that give you permission serve to encourage eating once the binge eater has started to eat. When the binge eventually ceases, negative emotions soon take over, including feelings of anxiety, regret and guilt for what they have done, as well as worry at the prospect of gaining weight as a result of their actions.

Purging

Binge eating may or may not be followed by self-induced vomiting or the misuse of laxatives or diuretics (water tablets) – this is called 'purging'. The various purging methods listed below are used to gain some kind of control over the possibility of weight gain as a result of the binge; however, they tend to be ineffective and are potentially dangerous. Some people purge because they feel the need to be punished for eating.

Making Yourself Sick

People with eating disorders feel anxious after eating, and some people feel the need to get rid of the food they have eaten in order to prevent themselves from gaining weight or, in some cases, to lose weight. For some people, self-induced vomiting – 'making yourself sick' in other words – can initially help relieve the fear of gaining weight. After vomiting, people often feel better at first for having got rid of the food; they're able to put their mind at rest, feel less anxious about their weight increasing, concentrate more clearly and get on with the day as usual. Rachel described her experience of vomiting as 'wiping the slate clean', and she was able to draw a line under her binges after promising herself that 'it would be the last time'. Other people beat themselves up after bingeing and vomiting, and felt regretful, shameful and disgusted with themselves, and this is likely to perpetuate the binge–purge cycle. People often feel hungry after purging as eating can trigger the binge–purge cycle once more.

People are often concerned that they might not be able to vomit up all the food they have consumed and so start the binge with a 'marker', such as beetroot or liquorice, or any food that they can easily identify when they make themselves sick. In fact, we know that this doesn't work because the contents of the stomach rotate and it's almost impossible to bring back all the food eaten. Digestion, especially of sugary things, takes place the moment food enters the mouth. We know that at least 50 per cent of the energy consumed in a binge is retained by our bodies.

Vomiting is usually achieved by sticking fingers or a toothbrush to the back of the throat. This triggers the gag reflex, the contraction of the diaphragm and abdominal muscles, which then force food upwards. Some people have become so practised at making themselves sick that just bending over is enough. Typically, self-induced vomiting lasts between five and thirty minutes and is repeated between one and ten times. Some people drink water, then vomit this back out to flush out their stomachs as completely as they think possible.

Facts about vomiting

1. Vomiting is not 100% effective at retrieving all the food you've eaten.
2. Vomiting will work against your efforts to stop bingeing because the more you binge and the larger the binge the more energy you will absorb and the more likely you are to gain weight.
3. After stopping vomiting some people gain weight BUT this is temporary and all fluid.
4. Vomiting causes a number of physical problems that include calluses on the back of the hands, swollen salivary glands that give you an appearance of a puffy face, sore throat, hoarse voice, stomach pains, acid reflux, thinning of enamel on your teeth and chipped teeth, imbalances in your blood chemistry.

Misuse of Laxatives and Diuretics

Misuse of laxatives and diuretics (commonly known as 'water pills') is also another form of purging.

People mistakenly believe these will help them control their weight but, in reality, this only causes the body to lose fluid. At first, getting rid of fluid relieves the body of the sensation of fullness and leads to feelings of emptiness, thinness and a belief that all the 'bad' food has passed through the body; however, the body quickly responds by retaining fluid, making the weight increase to a higher level than before.

Once a person begins to use laxatives as a form of weight control they gradually increase the dosage to achieve the desired effect and, when a person tries to stop taking these drugs, they often experience distressing withdrawal symptoms such as stomach cramps, bloating and constipation. It is always advisable to consult a doctor if you have any concerns about stopping the use of laxatives or diuretics.

Excessive Exercise

There are three key reasons why people choose to exercise: to control their mood (to relieve anxiety, stress, feelings of depression, agitation or unpleasant emotions); to control their weight (to lose weight, prevent weight gain, burn energy, to feel thin, to stop feeling guilty and to feel in control); for fun fitness and health reasons (to be physically healthy, to be active, for a sense of achievement to stay in a routine and to help with concentration). But exercise as a weight-management strategy can become excessive and, in some cases, compulsive, to the point where it can have a negative impact on a person's life.

Around 15 per cent of people who are considered to be a normal weight have 'exercise disorder', which involves compulsive exercise regardless of the circumstances (i.e., lack of time) or how people feel (i.e., if they are unwell). If interrupted from exercise, anger and irritation will follow. People tend to feel preoccupied with thoughts about exercising to the point of being distracted from other things and give exercise priority over other things such as relationships, work and family life. As with any compulsion, over time the amount of exercise required is increased to achieve the same effect.

Behaviours That Aim to Prevent Weight Gain

People with eating disorders often stick to strict routines to help themselves control their weight. Some people might have an exercise regime which they stick to on a daily basis. Megan, for example, would always start her day at 7.30 a.m. by jogging for 40 minutes because she felt the need to justify eating breakfast without feeling guilty. Regardless of what she ate, she would always follow this routine.

Chewing food and spitting it out is another eating disorder behaviour aimed at controlling weight. Matilda, a young mother with two young children, would normally restrict her intake of food but would work her way through several bars of chocolate over the course of an hour; she would put a chocolate in her mouth, suck and chew for a few seconds then spit it out without swallowing. She mistakenly believed she was getting a taste of the food she loved without it affecting her weight. What she did not realise was that she was still consuming some calories anyway as part of the process.

Psychological Problems Associated with Eating Disorders

So far we have discussed how eating disorders share similar features, such as worrying a lot about weight, shape, compulsive behaviour (constantly weighing yourself) and strict routines. We will now consider some of the common psychological problems associated with eating disorders.

Depression and Anxiety

We know that symptoms of depression and anxiety tend to increase during adolescence, especially for young women at the time of their first menstruation due to changes in their hormone levels and body shapes. Around 20 per cent of females at this time suffer from depression, substance abuse and relationship difficulties. Girls who have an early menstruation are at greater risk of developing an emotional problem than girls who begin to menstruate later. Research suggests there are three possible reasons for this: first, developing womanly physical characteristics such as breasts and round hips can increase the likelihood of being faced with new sexualised pressure and attention before the girl feels psychologically ready to deal with this; second, the dramatic physical changes that occur before other girls in the peer group can lead to social pressures that include being rejected and stigmatised; third, the girl may feel uncomfortable with an increase in body fat that moves her away from having the thin-ideal female body shape and this, in turn, can increase feelings of being unhappy with weight and shape.

Eating-disorder behaviours cause an enormous amount of upset, and it is often unclear if these lead to feelings of depression or if depression leads to eating disorders. The two problems tend to develop side by side but become less problematic once a pattern of regular eating is adopted. (If depression is a problem for you, I would suggest reading

Overcoming Depression by Paul Gilbert. See 'Other Things That Might Help' at the back of this book.)

Most of us will remember feeling shy, self-conscious and embarrassed as teenagers, blushing, stumbling over words and feeling socially awkward. These kinds of anxiety typically develop during our teenage years and are keenly felt by many people with eating disorders, who fear being judged negatively on the basis of their appearance or performance and will either avoid these situations altogether or put safety measures in place as a protection. Fortunately, many of us grow out of this and begin to feel more certain about ourselves and more confident. (For further information on social anxiety, I'd suggest reading *Overcoming Social Anxiety and Shyness* by Gillian Butler. See 'Other Things That Might Help' at the back of this book.)

We know that as people with eating disorders lose weight they become more obsessive and fixed in their ways and need to follow strict routines such as eating the same food at the same time each day to manage their anxiety. Many people with eating disorders, in particular anorexia, can often develop what is known as obsessive-compulsive disorder, or OCD. (For further information on OCD, I'd suggest reading *An Introduction to Obsessive-Compulsive Disorder* by Lee Brosan. See 'Other Things That Might Help' at the back of this book.)

Drug and Alcohol Use

The use of drugs and alcohol often coexists with an eating disorder. A study that looked at binge drinking and the use of recreational or 'party' drugs such as Ecstasy or cocaine in a group of people with anorexia and bulimia revealed that 15 per cent of those in the anorexia nervosa group and 30 per cent of people in the bulimia nervosa group had a drinking binge at least twice a week. For recreational drug use, 8 per cent of people in the anorexia group and 15 per cent in the bulimia group reported using recreational drugs at least twice a week. Drugs and the use of alcohol were often used to cope with eating disorder concerns, for example substituting alcohol for food.

2

Why Do Some People Develop Eating Disorders?

Plenty of theories have been put forward about the influences that might cause eating disorders but, unfortunately, the bottom line is that there is no agreement about why eating disorders occur. Eating disorders are complex and their development is thought to be influenced by environmental, genetic and psycho-social factors, as well as personality.

What we do know is that there are a number of different reasons for the development of eating disorders and that it isn't just a modern problem – historical accounts of eating disorders go back hundreds of years. Nowadays, we look at a combination of: (1) the risk factors that make people vulnerable to developing an eating disorder; (2) what triggers an eating disorder; and (3) behaviours and habits that keep it going. Along with these, we also look at our biological make-up – the things we have inherited through our genes – and the development of our social and psychological perspectives.

Risk Factors

We will now touch briefly on some of the risk factors.

Eating Disorders in Families

We know that eating disorders tend to run in families, which is not due to the inheritance of any one gene. (Genes carry information that determines the traits we have, such as our eye colour or aspects of our personality. These features are passed on to you by your parents.)

Scientists think there is complicated interaction between many genes that makes some people vulnerable to developing an eating disorder. If your mother or a sister has an eating disorder, you are twelve times more likely to develop anorexia and four times more likely to develop bulimia than someone whose immediate family does not have an eating disorder. Scientific evidence has shown that identical twins run a greater risk of developing the disorder than do non-identical twins, but also that brothers, sisters and families of twins with eating disorders have a greater rate of eating disorders compared to the rest of the population. Different types of eating disorders can develop within the same family.

Right now, scientists around the world are investigating whether there's a particular gene for each kind of eating disorder. But it's likely that the cause will include a variety of factors, not just genetic, especially as we know that children are influenced by and learn about eating behaviour and attitudes to food from their parents.

Being Female and the First Period

It is very normal for women to gain weight when they start their periods and then begin to feel some dissatisfaction with how they look. These concerns tend to persist and, for a time, become slightly worse. They develop alongside a number of other common psychological changes including greater levels of anxiety, especially in social situations, low self-esteem and feelings of being out of control. Many young women who are at a normal weight see themselves as overweight or even fat and will choose to diet and exercise excessively to try to change their body shape and weight.

Vulnerable Groups

People who engage in competitive physical activity and sports generally are at greater risk of developing an eating disorder and have higher rates of body dissatisfaction. This is particularly true if the sportsperson believes that reducing their body weight will increase their performance – such as footballers, jockeys or runners, for example; or when a certain body type is associated with high performance – such as wrestlers, rowers, gymnasts or swimmers. People whose sport has an aesthetic component such as dancers or ice skaters are also at risk.

Early Childhood

Sometimes, events that occur in childhood might have an impact on and influence how people react to and cope with events later in their life. For instance, the relationship between a parent and child is interrupted if there is a death or divorce in the family, or the relationship may be affected by the prolonged illness of a parent or other family member, who may require a great deal of care and attention. Parents might also need to work long hours or spend large periods away from home and, if parents have serious alcohol or drug-addiction problems or chronic psychiatric illnesses, they may at times seem to be uncaring and indifferent. Additionally, a proportion of people with eating disorders have suffered from a trauma such as bullying or physical or sexual abuse. It is also clear that a number of young people have been sexually exploited by adults and, without doubt, this increases their vulnerability to mental illness in general. These experiences can affect psychological development and increase susceptibility to eating disorders.

In some families, an unhealthy emphasis is placed on the significance of food and eating. Likewise, sometimes a child might never have seen 'normal' eating or, if there were regular mealtimes, they might have been surrounded by conflict. Food might be used as a reward or a punishment. And dieting might be encouraged even if it isn't necessary. Jaya's mother had body image issues and was always on the latest diet. Jaya gained a little weight during puberty and, although she was a healthy weight, her mother frequently told her she was fat and put her on a diet when it wasn't really necessary; from then on, they dieted together, which became the norm.

Socio-Cultural Influences

Social media websites such as Facebook and Instagram that portray images of 'thin-ideal, beautiful people' are thought to have a negative impact on some people and can lead to a momentary increase in feeling dissatisfied with their bodies. But does social media cause eating disorders? The simple answer is no, but social media for some people may play a part along with other psychosocial, biological and environmental factors. Being exposed to celebrities who are unrealistically thin, airbrushed and glammed up to the nines at a time when the gap between our actual body size and the cultural ideal is getting wider does not help when comparing how we think we look to our thin-ideal image.

What Triggers an Eating Disorder?

Many people with eating disorders have said that, at first, their weight loss or attempts to lose weight were due to stress such as school exams, a sporting event, leaving home, going to university, the death of a parent, the start of a relationship, worry about body image, being criticised about their weight and shape or having a viral illness. Of course, these events are a part of life, but not everyone develops an eating disorder because of them. In some ways, it's not the event itself – it's how we think about the event that determines our reaction.

Let's look at the following example of two ways to view such an event: imagine for a moment going to a family gathering and a relative tells you look fantastic and a picture of health. What goes through your mind? How do you feel? There are many possible ways of interpreting this. You might find yourself thinking, 'I must have gained weight ... they think I'm fat,' which is likely to make you feel pretty miserable. But you could also think, 'I'm quite pleased with how I look ... what a lovely compliment.' It's important to remember that there are different ways of interpreting events, and many of them have to do with self-confidence. (See *Overcoming Low Self-Esteem* by Melanie Fennell.)

Behaviour That Keeps the Eating Disorder Going

There are many reasons why eating disorders are maintained, but one of the reasons is that the people who suffer from the disorder have difficulty deciding whether it is 'friend or foe' and so feel torn about overcoming the problem. Eating disorders serve a function, such as helping a person believe that having the disorder will prevent parents from separating when they otherwise would have done so, or a way of providing protection from failure, or not having to face the demands of growing up and the challenges that brings.

The binge–purge cycle of bulimia nervosa allows people with the disorder to cope with negative feelings; however, bingeing and purging ultimately lowers mood and self-esteem and increases the likelihood of further binges.

Overall, and from the start, the initial weight loss provides a sense of achievement and satisfaction, but it is only short term, partly due to the physical effects of semi-starvation, which is followed by an increased preoccupation with food and eating. In turn, this becomes associated with control behaviours such as calorie counting, checking weight and scrutinising the body. Ironically, the stricter the measures of control, the greater the sense of feeling out of control, and this encourages an even stricter weight-loss strategy. This cycle is reinforced further by feelings of fullness when eating even small amounts that is interpreted as, 'I don't need to eat if I'm feeling full' or 'I can only eat when I'm hungry'.

Have I Got an Eating Disorder?

Researchers from the UK developed a screening tool for detecting eating problems in primary care (to be used during a consultation by a GP, family doctor or physician). It's called the SCOFF, which is an acronym with each letter representing one of five questions. You need to answer yes or no to each question, and every yes answer equals 1 point:

S	Sick – Do you make yourself sick because you feel uncomfortably full?
C	Control – Do you worry that you have lost control over how much you eat?
O	One stone – Have you recently lost more than 1 stone (14lb or 6.5kg) in a three-month period?
F	Fat – Do you believe yourself to be fat when others say you are too thin?
F	Food – Would you say food dominates your life?

If you have scored 2 points or more, then this indicates that you are quite likely to be suffering with an eating problem and should seek advice from a qualified health professional.

3

Treatment

Eating disorders are complex psychological disorders and psychological therapy is the recommended treatment of choice. There are many different types of treatments that help people overcome their problems with eating, and include family therapy (particularly helpful for younger people with eating disorders who are living at home), cognitive analytic therapy (CAT), interpersonal psychotherapy (IPT), focal psychodynamic therapy and cognitive behaviour therapy (CBT), which is the recommended treatment of choice for BN and BED.

This book is an introduction that will help you make a start on making some changes to your problems with eating and is based on CBT, which focuses on how you think (cognitive), how you feel and what you do (behaviour). For example, if after eating a meal you think, 'I shouldn't have had that, I'm out of control, I'll gain weight,' you may feel anxious and guilty and may behave in a way that involves skipping the next meal, checking your weight and body shape and restricting what you eat. This, in turn, can lead to further concerns about weight and shape and, before you know it, you can find yourself caught in a vicious circle.

You may choose to deal with the disorder yourself, or ask for the help of your family, a friend or health professional. You may find that, having made a start to understanding your eating problem, you now need to talk to your doctor about seeing someone who can help you to recover and become healthy again. It takes a lot of courage to ask for help and I hope you feel encouraged by reading this book to do so.

In Part 2 of this book there are several written exercises, with completed examples to guide you. It may be helpful to write things down in a notebook, or on a computer, smartphone or tablet, where you can keep a record of your thoughts, feelings, behaviours and progress.

A Word of Caution

Your safety is of the upmost importance. If any of the following apply to you it is important that you seek advice from your doctor before starting the programme:

1. You have lost weight rapidly
2. Your BMI is low (less than 17.5)
3. You feel faint, dizzy and your muscles feel weak
4. You are making yourself sick after eating
5. You are suffering from a medical condition such as diabetes
6. You are pregnant
7. You are feeling suicidal

Part 2: COPING WITH EATING DISORDERS

4

Motivation

Why now? What has made you decide to do something about your eating problems now? Take a moment and think about the advantages and disadvantages of having the eating disorder. After you have written things down, look at all the pros and cons. Simply doing this is a positive first step towards dealing with your eating disorder.

It's a fact that people with eating disorders believe there are advantages of having the disorder. Samantha felt very conflicted between believing that her eating disorder served a helpful purpose and, at the same time, knowing it caused her no end of problems. She is beginning to understand that making any change to her behaviour would be difficult and frightening, even though it is something she wants to do.

The next exercise will help you think about the advantages and disadvantages of changing.

Practical Exercise 1

First, jot down in your notebook some of the things you think are the advantages of having an eating disorder. If you're struggling to think of any pros, ask yourself what you would find difficult if someone waved a magic wand and suddenly took your eating disorder away.

Next, think about the disadvantages of your eating disorder. What don't you like about it? How does it affect you, your work, your relationships?

Now weigh up the advantages and disadvantages and make a note of what you have learned through doing this exercise.

To help you complete this exercise, look at Samantha's completed worksheet:

Samantha's Worksheet 1: Advantages and Disadvantages of Having an Eating Disorder

Advantages	Disadvantages
• I can eat what I want and not gain weight • It's familiar and in some ways it's easier to be bulimic, maybe I should just accept this is the way I am • Bingeing helps me cope with feeling anxious • It makes my boy-friend feel needed, he's always trying to help, I really feel cared for • If my exams don't go well I have an excuse	• At times it feels like my eating disorder is controlling my life; I'm sick of it • In reality it makes me feel completely miserable and alone • I'm unable to enjoy food like other people • I've hardly any friends because all my time is spent either bingeing and throwing up or exer-cising like mad • Physically I feel rubbish, my throat is permanently sore and I sound like I smoke twenty ciga-rettes a day • I'm always broke, all my money goes on food

Summary

 **What have I learned from doing this exercise?**

I didn't think there were any advantages to having bulimia and I'm surprised by how many answers I came up with. It makes sense to me why I have found making changes difficult. In reality I hate having bulimia.

Practical Exercise 2

In your notebook, jot down what you think some of the advantages of *changing* your eating disorder would be. Think about what you'd like to change and the most important reasons why you'd like to make those changes.

The next step is to jot down the disadvantages of making changes. What would concern you the most? What do you fear might happen?

Complete the two columns, then take some time to think about what you've learned from this exercise.

And on this worksheet, there's a 0 to 10 scale so that you can measure how you're feeling about it all. How much do you want to change right now? How ready do you feel for change? How willing are you to change?

Again, Samantha's worksheet is included as an example.

Samantha's Worksheet 2: Advantages and Disadvantages of Changing	
Advantages	**Disadvantages**
• I will feel better physically – I'll have more energy, and won't have any more sore, hoarse throats. My hair will become thicker because it'll stop falling out • I'd probably feel less anxious and depressed • If I weren't so concerned about eating alone so that I could binge alone I'd be more comfortable with other people and would probably have more friends than I do now • I'd have more time to think about my work and music • I'd be able to spend money on other things than food	• I'll gain weight and get fat • I'll have difficulty restraining myself and will lose control over eating • I'll end up substituting one eating disorder behaviour for another • My anxiety attacks won't go away if I don't binge and I'll come across to others as barking mad • My boyfriend will dump me

Summary

 **What have I learned from doing this exercise?**

Seeing the pros and cons of changing has helped me recognise there are more advantages to changing than not. The fact is that my fears about what might happen if I stop may or may not be true but I'll never know unless I try and give it a go.

✍ **Ask yourself the following three questions and circle the number that reflects how you feel right now.**

1. How much do I want to change?

0 1 2 3 4 5 6 7 8 9 10

Not at all Convinced

2. How ready do I feel?

0 1 2 3 4 5 6 7 8 9 10

Not at all Convinced

3. How able do I feel?

0 1 2 3 4 5 6 7 8 9 10

Not at all Convinced

It's normal to feel a little scared and you may still have some doubts about making changes. It's also important to find someone you like and trust to help and support you with the journey ahead.

5

Self-Monitoring

Observing and recording what you're doing, thinking and feeling will help identify exactly what is happening on a daily basis and is a helpful step towards overcoming your disorder. These kinds of observations and recordings are called 'self-monitoring' and will help make you more aware of your habits and help you to question and make changes to problematic thoughts and behaviours as they happen. We've included a self-monitoring sheet here for you to copy and fill in.

You may find the idea of self-monitoring boring and repetitive or feel worried that keeping such a record will make you feel worse when you're already thinking about food and eating most of the time. Indeed, you may find that for the first week or so that you think about food and eating more than usual but, once you get used to keeping a diary, you will find the advantages outweigh the disadvantages. At the very least, it's worth a try!

To give you ideas of how to self-monitor, the real-life self-monitoring sheets of Rachel and Megan can be seen below:

Tips for Self-Monitoring

- Use a self-monitoring sheet each day rather than a notebook or standard diary.
- Always keep your daily self-monitoring sheet with you.
- Record the information on a moment-by-moment basis while it is fresh in your mind; if you leave it until the end of the day you'll be unlikely to remember all the important details.
- Try to be honest and record things as they are no matter how embarrassed or ashamed you may feel.

Rachel's Self-Monitoring Sheet					
Time	**Food and Drink Consumed**	**Place**	**Excessive**	**Vomit/ Laxative**	**Comments**
7.30 a.m.	Black coffee x 1	Kitchen			Weight: 56kg up by 1kg! Feel fat and bloated after bingeing last night. I'm out of control.
8.00 a.m.	2 pints of water	Kitchen			Feeling hungry so drink water. Decide to go for a 45-minute run.
9.30 a.m.	Apple and small punnet of blueberries. Black coffee x 2	Kitchen			Feel hungry and tempted to have a slice of fruit loaf but resist. I'm not going to binge today!
12.30 p.m.	Tuna salad. Slice of apple pie with cream	Library café with friends	*	V V	Having the apple pie was too much. I could picture it sitting in my stomach and started to worry that I'd gain weight. I had to get rid of it then managed to carry on working in the library.

5.15 p.m.	Punnet of raspberries and a large pot of strawberry yoghurt	Bedroom	*		Feeling stressed about my exams and went to the supermarket on the way home to buy fruit and yoghurt then ate until the food ran out. I feel repulsive. No more food today, I'll start afresh tomorrow.
5.20 p.m.	A large bag of Maltesers with a banana milkshake	Bedroom	*		
5.30 p.m.	2 tubs of Ben and Jerry's ice cream Cherry Garcia and Cheesecake Brownie	Bedroom	*	V	
7 p.m.	A pint of water and a cup of green tea Bowl of cereal x 2 Toast with peanut butter x 6 Ham slices x 1 packet Chocolate digestive x 1 packet	Bedroom	* * *	V	I can't help it, I'm out of control. I'll end up the size of a whale. I hate myself. I need to take drastic action! Fast – just water.

Megan's Self-Monitoring Sheet

Time	Food and Drink Consumed	Place	Excessive	Vomit/ Laxative	Comments
8.00 a.m.	1 small bowl of skimmed milk and porridge with a small banana and flax seeds Green tea x 2	Kitchen			Weight: 50kg – same as yesterday, could be less though. Feeling hungry and ready for breakfast. I won't eat if I don't feel hungry.
1.00 p.m.	Tuna mayo sandwich – half a small tin of tuna, 1 teaspoon of 0-fat mayo and 1 medium slice of brown seeded bread 2 glasses water 1/2 punet 50g blueberries	Staff room			Really busy at work and stressed. I'm not hungry and don't want to eat and this feels like too much. I've removed the crust from the bread but I feel fat after eating and sick. What if I've gained weight???

3.00 p.m.	Black tea x 2 and 8 seed-less grapes. 5 almonds	Staff room			Felt okay eating grapes, I quite like the sugar rush – it gives me energy to get through the afternoon.
6.30 p.m.	Steamed vegetables– mangetout, green beans, broccoli. Small packet of prawns 2 glasses water	Kitchen			I'm ready to eat now, I'm a bit more relaxed and I've been able to control throughout the day. This meal is what I've eaten definitely justified.
9.00 p.m.	Low-fat hot chocolate with water	Living room			This will help me sleep. A good day, I'm feeling in control.

There are some instructions here for you to follow as you fill in your own self-monitoring sheet – the example is provided below for you to copy. Have a go at doing this for a week before moving on to the next exercise.

Instructions for Self-Monitoring

- Column 1 – Record the time you eat or drink anything.
- Column 2 – Write down a brief and clear account of what you had to eat or drink, e.g. 1 small packet of crisps, or two small Cox apples. You do not need to be too precise by recording the weight or brand of food; for example, if you ate a 30g bowl of a particular muesli, simply put down 'a small bowl of muesli'. Calories should not be recorded.
- Column 3 – Record where you were when you ate or drank anything. It's better to say 'dining room' than just 'home'.
- Column 4 – If you thought what you ate was excessive and would have rather not eaten, place an asterisk in the column. There are two reasons why you may regard food as excessive: it may be the type of food (for example, if it was

deep fried); or it may be the amount of food (for example, a large bowl of pasta when you had planned to eat a small portion). Deciding what is excessive is entirely up to you and it doesn't matter what anyone else thinks. Please record all the food you ate in a binge.

- Column 5 – In this column, record if you vomited (V) or used laxatives or diuretics (L).
- Column 6 – The comments column can be used in a variety of ways, for how you feel at the time of eating, particularly after episodes of eating you consider to be excessive. Remember to jot down any important circumstances that may have had an effect on your eating, and any thoughts and feelings you experienced. This may include social pressure to eat or a minor disagreement with a friend or feelings of frustration or boredom. This information is crucial to helping you understand some of the reasons why you restrict what you eat, or why you have episodes of excessive eating.

After you've monitored your eating for a week, it's time to review what you've learned. Here's an exercise that will help you do this.

Self-Monitoring Worksheet

Date__________ / Time__________

Time	**Food and Drink Consumed**	**Place**	**Excessive**	**Vomit/ Laxative**	**Comments**

Practical Exercise 3 – Reviewing Your Self-Monitoring Sheets

- Review the week's worth of self-monitoring sheets as a whole.
- What has gone well for you this week?
- What have you learned through reflecting on your self-monitoring sheets? (E.g., the circumstances that are likely to trigger a binge or make you decide to skip a meal.)
- What positive changes have you managed to make?
- What have you found difficult?
- Are these periods linked to binge eating, or a feeling of being out of control and a fear that you might gain weight?
- When tough things happen during the week, how does this influence your eating?
- How might you deal with this the next time you're faced with a similar situation?
- What CBT strategies can you use?
- What's your plan of action?

Building in a weekly review of your self-monitoring sheets and reviewing these questions will help you understand more about the nature of your eating problem. This will allow you to make important changes.

Self-Monitoring Worksheet

Date__________ / Time__________

Time	Food and Drink Consumed	Place	Excessive	Vomit/ Laxative	Comments

6

Meal Planning

This next stage of treatment involves learning to eat regularly. From now on, it will be important to eat three meals and three snacks a day. You may find this frightening and worry that you'll become fat and, indeed, if your weight is on the low side and below the recommended healthy BMI, it is likely that you'll gradually gain a small amount of weight but not enough to make you fat. Regular meals should include:

- Breakfast
- Mid-morning snack
- Lunch
- Afternoon snack
- Dinner
- Evening snack

Tips for Learning to Eat Regularly

- Each day you should try to eat three meals and three snacks according to a predetermined plan rather than waiting until you feel hungry. Having an eating disorder can make it difficult for people to recognise natural feelings of hunger or fullness, which can be confusing when deciding when and what to eat.
- Plan what you are going to eat a day at a time.
- You need to allow your body and mind to get used to eating regularly. At first, you may feel anxious about trusting the sensation of feeling hungry or not, because this is what your body has learned during the course of the disorder.
- Establish a pattern of eating first. As you become used to this you can then start to make changes to what you eat.
- Try and stick to the plan, do not eat in-between meals and snacks.
- Try not to go more than 3–4 hours without eating, even if this feels uncomfortable.
- Avoid vomiting or taking water tablets or laxatives.
- Always know roughly when and what you are going to eat in advance and eat at these times whether you are feeling hungry or not.

To give you an idea of what a meal plan might look like, here's a real-life example from Rachel's self-monitoring sheet:

7.30 a.m.	small bowl of cereal with milk and a piece of fruit
10.30 a.m.	a banana and a yoghurt
1.00 p.m.	a medium jacket potato with tuna and sweetcorn and a side salad
4.00 p.m.	an apple and a small handful of nuts
7.30 p.m.	salmon steak, three new potatoes, six asparagus spears
10.30 p.m.	a cereal bar and a hot chocolate

This is pretty much the type of plan you need to be aiming for each day. If you have severely restricted your food and the prospect of introducing three meals and three snacks a day feels alarming, try introducing the meal plan in stages. It can be helpful to think of the day in three parts: morning, afternoon and evening. At which time of the day do you find it easiest to eat? Which is the most difficult time? If you feel most comfortable eating in the morning, start by having breakfast and a mid-morning snack and jot down how you feel on your self-monitoring sheet.

Over the course of two to three weeks, and as you get used to eating more regularly, gradually build up to the full plan of three meals and three snacks a day. Bear in mind also that if you're having low-energy food – i.e., salad and vegetables – it can be counter-productive to keep your body in a state of semi-starvation and therefore prone to bingeing.

Gradually try to introduce a broader variety of food into your eating plan. One way to do this is to make a list of all the foods you enjoyed before your disorder began. Try to arrange the list into a ladder, with the foods you may find easiest to eat at the bottom and foods you might find difficult at the top. Starting from the bottom, reintroduce these foods, one at a time, back into your meals.

It's also a good idea to come up with several different options for each meal and to record these on index cards. If eating the same type and amount of food is a problem for you this will help you to introduce greater variety. Megan completed this exercise and an example of her ladder can be seen below.

Megan's Food Ladder	
Fish and chips and deep-fried food Indian and Chinese food Chocolate and puddings Pastry of any description	**Difficult**
Sausages Red meat – lamb, pork and beef Mayonnaise – full-fat Butter	**Easy to Difficult**
Croissant, pain au chocolat Pizza Bread Pasta	**Easier**

Healthy Eating for Weight Maintenance

After you've introduced three meals and three snacks a day and provided your BMI is more than 19, you may wonder what and how much you should be eating from now on. The Hand Jive, suggested by Dr K. Mawji, provides an imaginative way of estimating portion sizes for each meal based on the size of your hands:

The Hand Jive

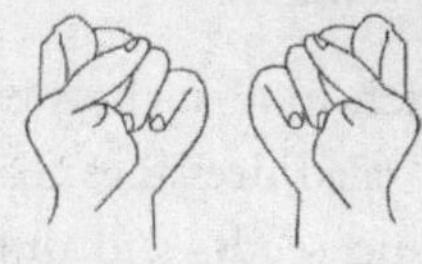

Your carbohydrate portion (i.e., potatoes, pasta, rice, bread) is the size of two fists

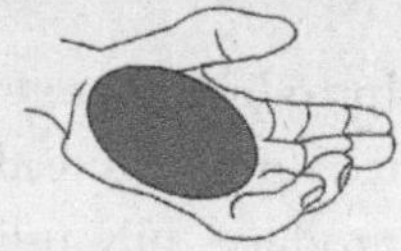

Your protein portion (i.e., fish, chicken, red meat, tofu, eggs, cheese) is the size of your palm and the thickness of your little finger

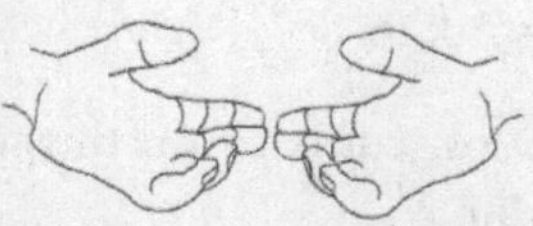

Your vegetable portion (i.e., salad, cabbage, broccoli, green beans, spinach but not potatoes) is the size of both hands

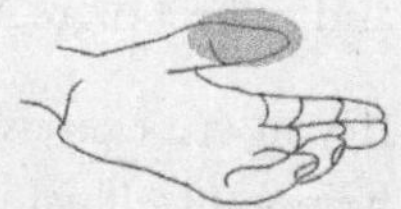

Your fat portion (i.e., mayonnaise, butter) is the size of your thumb

Regaining Weight If Your BMI Is Below 19

Regaining weight is an important part of overcoming an eating disorder, and a recommended weekly weight gain is 0.5kg a week. In order to achieve this, you'll need to increase your energy intake and there are a number of ways you can do this:

1. Have bigger portions of the same food. (Note, though, that if you are mainly eating low-energy food such as salad and vegetables, it may be almost impossible to eat the volume of food required to increase your weight.)

2. Introduce more energy-rich food such as butter on your bread, oil in salad dressings, dairy produce, oily fish, nuts and seeds, and drinks such as smoothies or milk shakes. The advantage of this is that you don't have to eat large quantities and you will be less likely to have the discomfort of feeling full.

3. Join in with social situations and celebrations and, when there, eat as others do.

4. If you are exercising a lot, cut back on this to help yourself gain weight.

If you are managing to gain a little weight each week, it means the changes you've made are working. If your weight stays the same or goes down over a period of 2–3 weeks it means the changes you are making are too small, even if you feel you're eating a lot more food and feel puzzled that your weight hasn't changed.

Be truthful with yourself. Are you playing it safe and under-eating? Or shaving a bit of food off other meals and snacks? Or skipping meals or snacks? Or increasing the amount of exercise you do? If so, it may be helpful to take some time, go back to your meal plan and self-monitoring sheet and review your thoughts. Look again at how you'd like to make some changes. It's not easy, and sometimes you have to try again before you get it going.

7

Coping with the Urge to Binge and Vomit

You may have found that starting to eat normally again and planning your meals has made a big difference to you and helped you feel a little better. Usually, once you feel less frightened about eating regularly and you've got used to eating three meals and three snacks a day, it's normal to notice that you binge less often; however, it's not always easy to stick to a meal plan and you might sometimes feel a powerful and overwhelming urge to binge. Changing your habits so that you begin to eat normally and regularly is not enough to help you stop bingeing altogether, especially since people often binge for psychological reasons that may be related to a situation you are finding difficult or that makes you feel anxious. Many of us find that eating can provide some comfort and help to ease our negative feelings when we are feeling this way, or when we're feeling bored or lonely. But these feelings of relief and comfort last for a short time only and, ultimately, bingeing will make you feel worse and make you want to binge yet again.

There's a great deal you can do to cope with the urge to binge – in part by finding ways to intervene when you spot the danger signs. Remember, though, that it's always possible to stop eating once you've started, even if you hadn't been able to stop yourself from starting and suddenly find yourself in the middle of a binge. It isn't always possible to be tuned into the danger signs.

The first step towards intervention is to review your self-monitoring sheets and ask yourself:

- Is there any regular pattern to my bingeing?
- When am I most likely to binge?
- How do I feel during these times?
- When I've resisted the urge to binge, what did I do that was helpful?

By asking yourself these questions you may start to understand a bit more about your urge to binge. Here are a few strategies that may help you cope with this urge:

Ten Tips for Coping with the Urge to Binge

1. Only eat in one place. If you binge in specific places such as the kitchen or the bedroom, try to ban yourself from eating in these places that you associate with bingeing. Sometimes, the urge to binge can be triggered by just being in these places. Try to think of a place where you don't binge and change it so you eat there instead.

2. Replace picking at food with chewing gum. Many of us find that when we prepare food for ourselves and for others we tend to pick at it, and this can increase the urge to binge. Sometimes chewing sugar-free gum can help you to stop picking.

3. Don't watch TV or read while eating. Research suggests that we eat much faster and more when we are distracted by watching the TV or reading. If you tend to have TV dinners, it's more likely that you'll have an urge to binge. If, instead, you sit at the table and take your time to eat slowly and mindfully, you may find this urge goes away. Having a family dinner or eating with others you feel comfortable with can help you to

slow down your pace of eating. However, if eating socially makes you feel anxious, have a go at eating alone and without any distractions. We tend to eat finger food (such as a slice of pizza) quickly, so try eating food (even if it is a slice of pizza) with a knife and fork.

4. Plan what to do after you've eaten, even before you start eating. Many of us find that at the end of a meal we still feel hungry and are tempted to eat more, which can then easily make us feel overfull and bloated. For many, these feelings increase the urge to binge. It's important to try to stick with what's on your meal plan and to have a clear plan about what you can do once you've finished eating; for example, not going into the kitchen immediately afterwards or doing something that doesn't involve food, such as watching the TV, reading a book, going on the Internet, listening to music, going for a walk or phoning/texting/emailing friends. Some people find that brushing their teeth with minty toothpaste at the end of a meal helps reduce the urge to binge.

5. Having a well-stocked larder and fridge can be extremely tempting when you have

a strong urge to binge. And it isn't great for you if the people you live with padlock the food cupboards or fridge as this will only serve to increase your urge to binge. If possible, try to restrict your supply of food to small quantities until you feel that you have more control over binge eating. This can be terribly inconvenient for you and for your family but it may be necessary and helpful to your recovery, especially in the early stages. Try to think of food planning in portions, such as a chicken leg rather than a whole chicken, or a slice of pizza rather than the whole thing. It can feel more manageable when there isn't the temptation of leftovers around. If bread is one of your binge foods, it can be helpful to keep the loaf of bread or rolls in the freezer and to defrost a portion at a time. Remember that it's not always possible for families to restrict food supplies if there are other members who need to be fed – for example, with packed lunches for siblings. So, another way to avoid having access to 'high risk' food in the house would be to place these in a container stored somewhere difficult to reach, such as the back of a cupboard. Doing this can act as a barrier to the urge to binge.

6. Always have a shopping list. When we feel hungry and shop we are likely to buy more food than we actually need and the type of food we crave and enjoy. Shopping with a list when you are not feeling hungry will help reduce your urge to binge. Shopping with a friend, if possible, can also help. Because of the secretive nature of binge eating, you are less likely to place food that you would binge on in your shopping trolley. Many people with eating disorders feel completely overwhelmed in food shops and can spend hours checking labels and feeling indecisive about what to buy. One way to overcome this, as well as unrestrained shopping, is to supermarket shop via the Internet and have your groceries delivered to your door; this way you are less likely to buy foods that you binge on.

7. Only carry the money you need. Armed with a debit/credit card or a purse full of money we can find ourselves making purchases impulsively. If you have a problem with binge eating and have money with you, your urge to binge is likely to increase when you are near food shops or vending machines. Practise taking out only the amount

of money you need and leave your cards at home. If you are buying petrol, go for the pay-at-the-pump stations, which will help you avoid the confectionery when you are queuing at the till.

8. Do not leave leftover food lying around. If we've enjoyed a meal, leftovers can seem like such a treat to enjoy later or something to savour later for those of us who hate the idea of wasting food. Leftovers can make us feel anxious and unsafe and trigger the urge to binge. The idea of throwing food away might feel wasteful, yet this is necessary until you feel able to control your binges. Many of us might convince ourselves that we will eat the leftovers for another meal but, if your urge to binge is strong, that is unlikely to happen. It can be helpful to throw leftovers away immediately after eating or to make the food inedible by putting washing up liquid on the food and scraping it into the bin.

9. Do not allow others to press food on you that you do not want. Many of us find that our friends and family love us to share a meal, especially during celebration feasts such as Christmas or Thanksgiving, or when it's easy to over-eat and have food that we

don't really want in order to be polite. Overeating can increase the urge to binge and it's important that you learn to be firm but polite and say no to offers of food or when you're feeling bullied to eat. It might be worth practising a few phrases to use in this situation. For example, 'The coffee-and-walnut cake was delicious but, right now, I feel full and can't manage another bite!' or 'No, thank you, not right now, maybe later, you go ahead and order dessert.'

10. Always follow your meal plan. Planning three meals and three snacks a day means you are always one step ahead and never need to go more than four hours without eating. When you have the urge to binge, it can be helpful to refer to your plan. Also think about how you will feel later if you manage to resist the urge to binge.

Alcohol

Many of us find that when we drink alcohol our appetite increases and we are more likely to nibble snacks and eat more than usual. And often the day after drinking alcohol we can feel ravenously hungry and crave certain foods. Drinking alcohol can reduce your resistance to binge eating so, if you can, try to drink alcohol in moderation.

How to Stop or Interrupt Bingeing

One of the most effective ways of stopping or interrupting a binge is using a binge-postponement strategy. If you tell yourself that you must or should not binge, this will make you want to do it all the more; with binge postponement, you're not telling yourself that you can't do it, you are telling yourself that you're just putting it off, or 'postponing' it until later. When you feel the urge to binge, tell yourself that you aren't going to binge for the next fifteen minutes, then distract yourself with an activity. After fifteen minutes have passed and if you still have an urge to binge, you then postpone bingeing for another fifteen minutes and continue with the same activity or move to the next one on your list until the urge to binge has gone completely. It can be helpful to prepare a list of things you can do instead of binge eating and, when you do so, it's important to consider:

- Activities that take you away from the place you usually binge

- Activities that are easy to do
- Activities that are positive and pleasurable
- Activities that involve using your hands
- Activities that engage your mind and require good concentration

To give you an idea, here's an example of Rupert's list of activities:

Rupert's Activities

- FaceTime/WhatsApp/text friends
- Browse Facebook and chat to friends
- Play my guitar
- Go out for a walk around the park
- Take a hot shower
- Watch YouTube or TV programme
- Seek out friends in the same halls of residence – i.e. drop in on Dillon, Maddy, Oli, Jamie or Sam
- Do some sketching
- Read a chapter from whatever novel I'm reading

Exercise – Alternatives to Bingeing

As part of your plan to cope with your urge to binge, make a note of activities you could do instead of binge eating and follow the example and guidelines listed above. If you still have a strong urge to binge, before eating anything write down what you plan to eat in a binge. Ask yourself, 'How will I feel if I binge? ... How will I feel if I don't binge? ... Do I still want to go ahead with this?'

Coping with the Urge to Vomit

If you manage to cope with your urge to binge and begin to binge less, it is likely that you'll feel less inclined to make yourself sick. Earlier, we discussed the binge-vomit cycle and how bingeing encourages vomiting and vomiting encourages overeating. Many people who binge believe they may as well eat large amounts of food to make vomiting worthwhile, or only feel able to vomit if their stomach is filled to capacity. But very shortly after vomiting, you are likely to feel hungry again and this can lead to further bingeing.

For some of us, especially if you're underweight, vomiting can become a habit and it's easy to believe that, unless you vomit after everything you eat, you'll gain weight and become fat – the number-one fear for people with eating disorders. After vomiting, the empty feeling may seem comforting and reassuring because you believe you will not gain weight. However, what often happens is that people who binge-purge start to feel increasingly uncomfortable with eating, and the feeling of having food in their stomach causes anxiety and distress about the feared consequences of bingeing – i.e., weight gain. This encourages a strong urge to vomit to compensate for having eaten a large amount of food.

It's possible to learn how to cope with the urge to vomit and to interrupt the binge-vomit cycle. Delaying tactics, like binge postponement, involve delaying vomiting for as long as you can after eating. It can be helpful to look at your self-monitoring sheets to find the timeframe between eating and making yourself sick. This can vary quite a lot; some people make themselves sick several times throughout a binge or at the end of a binge, while others will vomit after eating small amounts of food.

You may feel anxious and uncomfortable with feeling full when you begin to delay making yourself sick. In time, though, you'll find that you gradually feel less anxious and less uncomfortable after eating or when you feel full. When you have a strong urge to be sick, try to delay being sick with a five-minute gap between eating and being sick, then gradually progress to gaps of ten, fifteen, twenty, twenty-five minutes until the urge to vomit passes completely. If you do manage to resist the urge, then the next time you put this delay tactic into practice you may find that the urge to vomit passes more quickly. Similar to binge postponement, try to distract yourself with positive activities from your pre-planned list. Or try counting backwards from 100 in threes (100, 97, 94...), or describe an object, such as a chair, out loud.

If vomiting has become a habit and you are making yourself sick after almost everything you eat, then you can try to cope with the urge in stages. It can be helpful to divide your day into six parts: breakfast; mid-morning snack; lunch; mid-afternoon snack; dinner; and after-dinner snack. Decide which part of the day is easiest to keep food down, and which part of the day is the most difficult. For example, if you feel more comfortable keeping breakfast down, then this is a good place to start reducing how often you vomit. Plan your strategy and decide what you'll do to make yourself less inclined to be sick after eating breakfast. Rupert had a routine of eating breakfast in his room and, to help himself try to break his binge-purge cycle, he went to the university canteen instead for breakfast with his friends. He made a point of chatting for a while afterwards and this helped him keep his food down. Like Rupert, once you've managed to keep one meal down, you'll feel more confident about the others and you'll be more able to take charge of your eating disorder, instead of it taking charge of you.

It can be helpful to record on your smart phone or a small card some reassuring statements you can refer to when you have a strong urge to vomit, for example: 'Although I feel uncomfortable right now, these feelings will pass.' Remember to distract yourself from these feelings and select an activity from your list – think about how you will feel if you manage to keep the food down. Making changes is always a challenge but you *can* do it, even if it's very difficult and you find yourself trying and trying again.

The Fear of Eating Normally and Gaining Weight

It's easy to assume that vomiting is preventing you from becoming overweight and when you stop it's likely that your anxiety about gaining weight will increase. A common and strongly held belief is: 'If I eat normally (three meals and three snacks a day) like other people, I'll become overweight and fat.' On a scale of 0–10, with 10 meaning you're totally convinced this is true, how much do you believe this right now?

The truth is that if you are underweight (with a BMI of less than 19 – see Chapter 1), learning to eat normally again will mean that you will gain weight, but only gradually, and be restored to a normal and healthy range (BMI of 20–25), and *not* an overweight range (BMI 26–30).

Nobody can say for sure what will happen to your weight when you break the binge-vomit cycle and most of us find that a wait-and-see attitude can help us observe what happens and how you feel over time. It's normal to have an immediate increase in weight, especially if you have regularly binge-purged over a long period of time, and you may feel bloated, but remember this is fluid at first and not fat. Over time, your weight will stabilise.

8

Negative Thoughts and Eating Disorders

You have now learned to use self-monitoring to tune into your thoughts and feelings about eating, weight and shape concerns. Recognising your thoughts and feelings and how these affect what you do is an important step towards changing how you think. It can be helpful to recognise not just *what* you are thinking but *how* you are thinking and then learn to label certain types of thoughts so that you can see them in a different light. Listed below are some thoughts that many people with eating disorders seem to share. Go through the list and highlight any that may apply to you.

1. All or nothing thinking. You see things as black or white. There are no shades of grey; food is either good food or bad food. Breaking one of your rules about eating makes you throw in the towel for the rest of the rules: 'I've blown my eating plan by having an ice cream, so I might as well carry on eating.'

2. *Blowing things out of proportion or making things into a catastrophe*. In your mind, every small problem becomes a giant of a problem and feels impossible to overcome. After eating a piece of cake, you feel panicky and believe you are out of control.

3. *Over-generalisation*. One negative event is taken out of turn and makes you believe or think it's the start of an endless negative spiral, such as when you gain a small amount of weight and believe this is the pattern from now on, that you'll keep gaining weight and become fat.

4. *Labelling*. You relate to yourself in a scathing and critical way, calling yourself names like 'disgusting', 'a failure' or 'useless' and believe these labels sum you up.

5. *Mind reading and jumping to conclusions*. You believe you know what other people are thinking – mainly that it's always about you and that it's negative. You then react to what you imagine other people are thinking and jump to the wrong conclusions. You catch an attractive man's eye in a public place and think they are thinking you're fat and ugly and conclude they would never be interested in you.

6. Fortune telling. You look ahead to the future and think that what it holds is doom and gloom, without anything positive or happy on the horizon. This can lead to you feeling demotivated and hopeless.

7. Mental filter. You have an internal radar that hones in on and draws attention to your mistakes and weakness, filtering out the good things you have done. Linked to this is '*discounting the positive*', which is when you immediately counter anything positive that happens to you or is said about you with a negative. If someone gives you a compliment, you assume they are saying that just to be polite and don't really mean it.

8. Shoulds, musts and ought tos. You spend a lot of time telling yourself what you should do and must do, and falling short of these standards leads to self-criticism. This leaves little room for error and results in lowering your self-esteem.

9. Emotional Reasoning. You assume that feelings are factual. If you feel fat then you believe it's true that you have gained weight. If you feel anxious it means something bad is about to happen.

Challenging Negative Thinking

Negative thoughts are automatic and believable at the time we have them and rarely do we stop and question what we are thinking. When you look back over your self-monitoring sheets, how realistic do your negative thoughts seem to you now? When you have some distance from your thoughts you can see them with fresh eyes, and from a different perspective. You will learn how to challenge these thoughts by examining the evidence around them to help you decide if they are actually fair or realistic.

Learning to challenge negative thoughts is a skill that you will acquire with time, patience and practice. There are a number of steps to take. First, go back to one of your self-monitoring sheets and rate how much you believed each thought on a scale of 0–100 per cent, with 100 per cent meaning you were completely convinced the thought was true. Next, do the same to rate how strong your feelings about these thoughts were at the time and consider how much you believe the thoughts right now. See if you can identify any differences between the two. If so, you'll begin to understand that you're seeing your thought patterns from a different point of view. Try to remember how you feel now, so that the next time you have these negative thoughts, you can pause and look at them with a more realistic perspective. It can be helpful to capture and record thoughts as they occur and to challenge them there and then in the moment. However, at first when you are learning this skill, it might not be possible to challenge these thoughts straight away, especially if you are feeling very upset. If that's the case, it can be helpful to return to the self-monitoring sheet once you feel a little calmer and to challenge the thoughts then. This will help you develop the skills to be able later to challenge the negative thoughts as they occur. Rachel adapted her self-monitoring sheet to use it as a thought-challenging record, and it's been included here as an example of how you might challenge your own thoughts:

An Example of Extending Self-Monitoring to Challenge Negative Thinking

Situation	**Thoughts**	**Emotions 0–100%**	**Alternative thought 0–100%**	**Action Plan**
Where were you? What were you doing?	*What were you thinking?*	*How did you feel?* *How strong were your feelings on a scale of 0–100%?*	*What evidence does not support the thought?* *How much do I believe the alternative thoughts on a scale of 0–100%?* *What is another way of looking at the thought?* *After examining the facts re-rate the emotion*	*What can I do now? What's my plan?*
Eating in a restaurant with friends and deciding to have pasta.	I'll gain weight. (catastrophising) People will think I'm greedy. (mind reading)	Anxiety 90% Embarrassed 80% Sad 70%	It's unlikely eating a bowl of pasta will make me gain weight. Other people are eating the same and I don't think they will gain weight.	Plan – eat the pasta and continue with my eating plan. Observe my weight over the next 3 weeks.

			I don't know what other people are thinking; it's only me who remembers in detail what others are eating. (mental filter) Most people are interested in other things and what I'm eating is probably the last thing on their mind. If my friends did actually think I was greedy I'm not sure I would want them to be friends. Anxiety 20% Embarrassed 30% Sad 10%	Plan – Pay attention to the things I used to enjoy about going to a restaurant, the atmosphere, the conversation.

Testing Negative Thoughts

- In what way is this thought understandable?
- What are the facts of the situation?
- If you had a friend in a similar situation and they had this thought, what advice would you give them? What advice would a friend give to you?
- How would you feel if you were able to say those things to yourself?
- What are the advantages and disadvantages of thinking this way?
- How will you feel about the thought a week from now?
- What is another, more helpful way of looking at this thought?
- What can you do next? (Action plan)

Bear in mind that as you have probably been thinking this way for some time, you'll need to keep practising. If you continue to challenge your negative thoughts, you should start to notice a difference over the next few weeks.

A Few Words of Encouragement

This book provides you with information about eating disorders and introduces you to some strategies to help you get started on overcoming your eating disorder. These strategies focus on understanding your motivation for change and identifying the difficulties you may experience before you begin. Being able to self-monitor, structuring your meals and eating regularly, is central to recovery. The aim is to break the vicious circles that perpetuate your eating-disorder behaviours. It'll take time, and you may have to try again, but keep at it! And remember that help is always available from either your friends, family or from professionals. Asking for help is often difficult, and takes courage, but it is yet another step towards recovery.

9

Family and Friends

The final chapter in this book is for family and friends of someone with an eating disorder. You might have a son, daughter, spouse or good friend who you suspect is in the early stages of developing an eating disorder, or perhaps they have had an eating disorder for some time. We know that this can cause families an enormous amount of distress; it is emotionally demanding and challenging. Family members usually provide the main support and care for the person who suffers from the disorder but they are often unsure of the best thing to do. It is typical for parents to feel they are responsible for causing the eating disorder, and blame themselves for mistakes and think that their parenting abilities have not being good enough.

The truth is that *no one causes* eating disorders, which are serious mental health problems associated with significant physical complications. The person with an eating disorder didn't choose to have one and they didn't cause it themselves; it's a problem that is characterised by extreme anxiety and fear. Blaming yourself or the person with the eating disorder will only make you both feel worse than you do already. I've included a few links to more information on caring for someone with an eating disorder in the resource section that follows but, in the meantime, here are a few common concerns and some suggestions about how you may begin to help:

Someone I care for has an eating disorder but will not acknowledge there is a problem. What should I do?

It can be very frightening to see someone you care for struggling with an eating disorder and most of us would find that our natural instinct is to offer care and support and try to help them recover. However, when the person with the disorder doesn't recognise that they have a problem, they can become angry and irritated with you and your efforts to help. In this case, you should remember the three Cs: keep Calm, be Caring and show Compassion, which is about doing what is best for the person you care for through validating their feelings, yet at the same time being open and honest about your concerns, especially when you want to discuss the subject. You might want to say something like, 'I've noticed you seem to be struggling with eating and have lost weight ... I can see that things are difficult for you at the moment. Could we talk?' Again, it's important to remain calm when you move forward with the conversation. If you disagree at times, it's best to acknowledge this; for example, you might say, 'I can see that we have different views about what's happening with your health right now. Please understand that I feel extremely concerned that you've lost a lot of weight but I also respect the fact that you don't agree and you think I'm making a big fuss. I'll let it drop for now but I'm going to think about what you've told me and hope that you'll also think about what I've said. Perhaps we can meet somewhere in the middle. Let's talk about it again in a bit after we've both had some time to stand back and reflect. The bottom line is that I love you and I'm here to support you.'

You might feel frustrated that you do not see eye to eye, but you'll need to keep trying. Set small and gradual goals of what you can do to help the person you care for and recognise that they have a problem. And remember the three Cs – keep Calm, be Caring and show Compassion.

Should we see our family doctor?

Many people with eating disorders develop significant medical problems caused by malnourishment and being very underweight or because of frequent bingeing and self-induced vomiting. It is important that a doctor can assess all physical and psychological risks, and develop a picture of what is happening. At the very least, they should keep a regular check on their patient's physical health to make sure they are medically safe.

We know that people with eating disorders find it difficult to ask for help because they often feel ashamed and embarrassed, or they genuinely don't believe there is a problem and think that everyone is making a big fuss, which adds to their anxiety and fears. Many people with anorexia nervosa don't recognise they have a problem and have developed their own theory about what has caused their weight loss. It's easy to be drawn into accepting these genuinely held beliefs; try not to enter into a conflict and acknowledge each person's point of view. A compromise solution would be for the person to agree to see a professional for an independent assessment. However, bear in mind that not all doctors understand eating disorders so it's important to make an appointment with someone who has an interest in mental health problems. You can offer support by suggesting that you'll make the appointment to see the doctor and will go along with them if the person you are caring for finds this helpful.

How do I offer support at mealtimes?

One of the first aims of treating people with eating disorders is to help them establish a regular pattern of eating three meals and three snacks a day. Given how different this is to what they've become used to, it's normal for them to feel extremely anxious at the thought of this new routine. The type of support you are able to offer now is crucial to their recovery. You'll need to be consistent and firm, yet all the while remember the three Cs – Calm, Caring and Compassion.

When Emma began to eat regularly, she would be tearful at every mealtime and try to convince her parents that she didn't really need to eat, and she believed the meals were too much. She would lash out and accuse her parents of misunderstanding her and purposefully trying to make her fat when she saw herself as slim and of normal weight. But if the food plan is agreed on in advance, as it needs to be, it is important to stick to it. You might encourage someone like Emma by saying that the food is her medicine and that she has to eat (breakfast or her snack, for example), and that this is a step towards becoming healthy again. Remind her gently that you had all agreed on the plan and that you are there for her support. It is also helpful to let them know that you are aware of how they feel

– frightened or anxious – and that the process will be difficult but necessary and will eventually become easier.

Try to make mealtimes peaceful, maybe sit around the family table eating together and talking about the things you used to enjoy talking about, not the things you argue about. Try to avoid making comments about what the person is eating, or not – doing this is likely to make the situation worse. After mealtimes, it can be helpful to start another activity to distract everyone from the food issue – try watching TV, playing a board game, going for a gentle walk or telephoning a friend or relative.

The person I care for feels upset if I eat less than them, what should I do?

Our energy requirements are all different and if you are trying to gain weight you will need to eat much more than someone who is trying to keep their weight stable. You may need to explain this gently but also acknowledge that it must be difficult for them to have to eat more than others at the table. Gently remind them also that eating is a step towards recovery.

My daughter/son is binge eating and taking a large amount of food from the fridge and cupboards. What should I do?

It can be extremely frustrating and expensive if your weekly shop for the family disappears in a day and it's easy to argue about this and make threats such as putting a lock on the fridge door or demanding payment for the food. When Rachel was at university she would secretly binge on other people's food in the halls of residence. When the other students found their food was missing, they were furious, and posted unpleasant messages on the fridge door. Rupert would empty the fridge at home when bingeing and, on one occasion, ate the Easter eggs that belonged to his younger brother and sister, which made him hugely unpopular, as you can imagine.

But even if it may be understandably easy to argue, battling it out is usually unhelpful and can increase feelings of humiliation and guilt. People who binge feel unable to stop eating once they start and no one with bulimic problems feels good about taking food that doesn't belong to them. It's simply that they find the urge to binge so great that it overwhelms any other feelings of what is right or wrong. Yet, afterwards, they do feel terrible about what they have done. When Rachel ate other people's food, she would set her alarm early and dash to the supermarket to replace the food she had taken as a way of coping with her feelings of guilt and shame.

It can be helpful to discuss this openly and calmly – try to think of all the possible solutions to the problem. Rupert felt very unsafe with a lot of food in the house, in particular crisps and biscuits. His mother agreed to shop on a daily basis early on in his recovery so that the amount of fresh food in the house was limited. They would agree what his meal plan would be for the following day and they would shop accordingly, sometimes together. They also agreed to not have any sweets or crisps in the house. Once Rupert gradually managed to stop bingeing, in part by practising what he had learned from Cognitive Behaviour Therapy, they were able to bring increasing amounts of food back into the house.

Caring for someone with an eating disorder is exhausting. I don't feel that I have a life of my own any more.

Recovering from an eating disorder can take a long time and you must continue to care for yourself as well as the person you're looking after. It's a huge burden that takes a lot of mental and physical energy and can leave you feeling low. It might be worth thinking about the things you stopped doing when you began to care for someone with an eating disorder. Rupert's parents, for example, hadn't been out together as a couple for some time and family holidays had been put on hold. Rupert's father had stopped playing golf at the weekends and his mother rarely saw her friends, but putting their lives on hold didn't speed up Rupert's recovery and it won't speed up the recovery of the person you're supporting.

It's important for you also to have support from family and friends and try to remain as upbeat as possible. Notice how it feels when you return to doing the things you used to enjoy. You may feel a little anxious at first for not dedicating most of your time to caring for the person in recovery but, in time, you will feel much better for taking some time out for yourself. It's often helpful to talk to other people who are in a similar position and it might be worth considering going to a support group (see resources).

For those with further questions or concerns, the resources section at the back of this book offers a useful source of information for anyone suffering with an eating disorder, and for their families, carers and friends.

The Journey to Recovery

Your journey might feel like a long haul right now but complete recovery is possible for many people who suffer with an eating disorder. I hope this book has helped you make the first step but you may decide that you need to ask for professional advice. When you do this, remember to discuss with your doctor the options available to you and jot down all the things you'd like to talk about or have questions about before your appointment. This will help you to be prepared and to be clear about what it is that you may need, especially when you may feel anxious about talking these things over with a doctor. It may be helpful to take this book along.

It's a big, brave decision to take the plunge and ask for help. Your family and friends are there to support and care for you and want to be included. It's so important to your recovery that you allow them to help you.

I do hope this book has shed some light on the ways eating disorders come about, how they develop, and how they can begin to be overcome.

I wish you well on your road to recovery, one step at a time.

Other Things That Might Help

For Family, Carers and Friends

Anorexia and Bulimia in the Family: One Parent's Practical Guide to Recovery by Gráinne Smith (Wiley)

Anorexia Nervosa: A Recovery Guide for Families, Friends and Sufferers by Janet Treasure and June Alexander (Psychology Press)

(This is a new edition of the 1997 book)

Boys Get Anorexia Too: Coping with Male Eating Disorders in the Family by Jenny Langley (Paul Chapman Publishing)

Bulimia: A Guide for Family and Friends by Roberta Trattner Sherman and Ron Thompson (San Francisco: Jossey-Bass)

Eating Disorders: A Parents' Guide by Rachel Bryant-Waugh and Bryan Lask (Routledge)

Mealtimes and Milestones: A Teenager's Diary of Moving on from Anorexia by Constance Barter (Robinson)

Skills-Based Caring for a Loved One with an Eating Disorder: The New Maudsley Method by Janet Treasure, Gráinne Smith, Anna Crane (Routledge)

Skills-Based Learning for Caring for a Loved One with an Eating Disorder: The New Maudsley Method by Janet Treasure, Gráinne Smith, Anna Crane (Routledge)

Help Your Teenager Beat an Eating Disorder by James Lock and Daniel Le Grange (Guilford Press)

Surviving an Eating Disorder: Strategies for Families and Friends by Michele Siegel, Judith Brisman and Margot Weinshel (New York: Harper)

Self-Help Books for Bulimia Nervosa and Binge Eating

Beating Your Eating Disorder by Glenn Waller, Victoria Mountford and Rachel Lawson (Cambridge University Press)

Bulimia Nervosa: A Cognitive Therapy Programme for Clients – A Cognitive Manual by Myra Cooper, Gillian Todd and Adrian Wells (Jessica Kingsley)

Getting Better Bite by Bite: a Survival Kit for Sufferers of Bulimia Nervosa and Binge-Eating Disorders by Ulrike Schmidt and Janet Treasure (Psychology Press)

Overcoming Binge Eating by Christopher Fairburn (Guilford Press)

Overcoming Bulimia Nervosa and Binge Eating by Peter Cooper (Robinson)

Overcoming Weight Problems by Jeremy Gauntlett-Gilbert and Clare Grace (Robinson)

Self-Help Books for Anorexia Nervosa

Anorexia Nervosa: The Wish to Change by Carol Bowyer, A. H. Crisp, Christine Halek and Neil Joughin (Psychology Press)

Overcoming Anorexia Nervosa by Christopher Freeman (Robinson)

Online Resources

B-eat is a well-respected UK charity for people with eating disorders and their families and its website is packed full of useful information: *www.b-eat.co.uk*. The B-eat bookshop offers a range of self-help and information books that you can buy online. These include the charity's own publications for carers, teachers and parents. *www.b-eat.co.uk/shop/bookshop*. B-eat self-help groups are for carers and sufferers and meet regularly throughout the UK. Visit the beat website's HelpFinder directory for links to groups.

The National Eating Disorders Association NEDA – *www.nationaleatingdisorders.org* –provides help for carers and those who are affected by an eating disorder. The resources are extensive and I would recommend viewing the video clips that share valuable information about eating disorders. There is a downloadable toolkit for carers and detailed information for men and boys who suffer with an eating disorder.

The eating disorders research group at King's College has a very useful site: *www.kcl.ac.uk*. Once on the home page, type 'eating disorders' into the search bar, and you'll find the section developed by the eating disorders research team based at the Institute of Psychiatry in London, and it's full of excellent information. I would particularly recommend the information for carers section which has a downloadable information sheet, and also the resource section which has the 'Restoring Regular Eating' plan: three meals, three snacks. You can find it by typing 'restoring regular eating' into the search bar.

Professor Janet Treasure from the Institute of Psychiatry in London has produced a series of brilliant short animated films that are mainly aimed at helping people who are caring for someone with an eating disorder. The short films are between three and ten minutes long and give you lots of ideas about how to encourage motivation to change and how to talk to someone you are supporting who has an eating disorder. For those of you who are struggling to tell your friends that you are suffering with an eating disorder I would recommend the film, *Dude, Where's the Food? Explaining Eating Disorders to Friends*. To view these films log on to YouTube – *www.youtube.com* – and type 'CandMedProductions' into the search engine.

The Something Fishy website – *www.something-fishy.org* – is packed full of helpful information and I would recommend for carers the section from the drop-down menu on approaching someone you care about. The site also has excellent information from those of you who are suffering with an eating disorder. There is a chat room where you can talk to other people with eating disorders, carers and professionals.

The Canadian-based Mirror-Mirror website – *www.mirror-mirror.org* – has information on eating disorders and a particularly helpful section for carers on approaching someone you love who has an eating disorder.

Resources for General Mental Health Problems Common to Eating Disorders

The Royal College of Psychiatrists website – *www.rcpsych.ac.uk* – has some excellent downloadable information sheets about mental health problems.

The British Association of Behavioural and Cognitive Psychotherapies (BABCP) website – *www.babcp.com* – has information on Cognitive Behavioural Therapy (CBT) and an excellent range of information sheets that can be downloaded.

If you also have problems with depression, social anxiety and shyness, obsessive-compulsive disorder or alcohol I would recommend looking at some of the other books in the *Overcoming* series of CBT self-help programmes, which can be found at: *www.overcoming.co.uk*.

An Introduction to Coping with Phobias

2nd Edition

Brenda Hogan

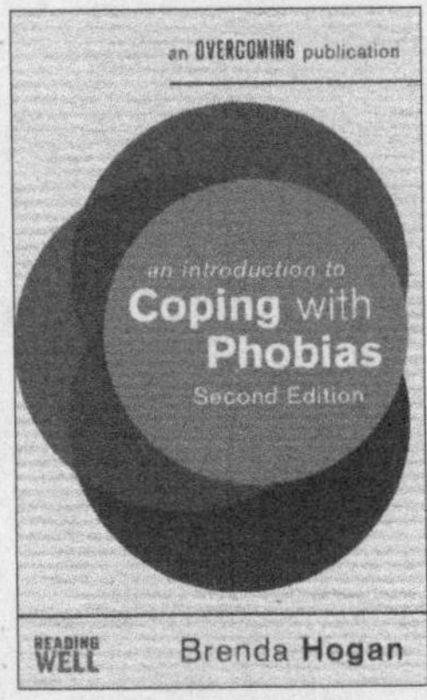

Available to buy in ebook and paperback

Learn how to overcome your phobias

It is very common for people to have a phobia of something – heights, spiders, water. . . but when that fear prevents you from doing the things you enjoy in life, or causes you deep anxiety and feelings of panic, it is time to seek help.

This self-help guide explains how phobias develop and what keeps them going. This updated edition gives you clinically proven cognitive behavioural therapy (CBT) techniques to help you challenge the way you think and behave in order to treat your phobias:

Set goals and start to face your fears

Avoid relapses and learn to problem-solve